RULES AND REGULATIONS

FOR THE

SWORD EXERCISE

OF THE

CAVALRY.

By His Majefty's Command.

Adjutant-General's Office,
1st December, 1796.

RULES AND REGULATIONS

FOR THE

SWORD EXERCISE

OF THE

CAVALRY

The Naval & Military Press Ltd

Published by the
The Naval & Military Press
in association with the Royal Armouries

Unit 10 Ridgewood Industrial Park,
Uckfield, East Sussex, TN22 5QE
Tel: +44 (0) 1825 749494
Fax: +44 (0) 1825 765701

MILITARY HISTORY AT YOUR FINGERTIPS
www.naval-military-press.com

ONLINE GENEALOGY RESEARCH
www.military-genealogy.com

ONLINE MILITARY CARTOGRAPHY
www.militarymaproom.com

The Library & Archives Department at the
Royal Armouries Museum, Leeds, specialises
in the history and development of armour
and weapons from earliest times to the
ROYAL present day. Material relating to the
ARMOURIES development of artillery and modern
fortifications is held at the Royal
Armouries Museum, Fort Nelson.

For further information contact:
Royal Armouries Museum, Library, Armouries Drive,
Leeds, West Yorkshire LS10 1LT
Royal Armouries, Library, Fort Nelson, Down End Road, Fareham PO17 6AN

Or visit the Museum's website at
www.armouries.org.uk

*In reprinting in facsimile from the original, any imperfections are inevitably reproduced
and the quality may fall short of modern type and cartographic standards.*

Printed and bound by CPI Antony Rowe, Eastbourne

Adjutant General's Office,
1st December, 1796.

Tʜᴇ following Rules and Regulations for the Sword Exercife, are, by His MAJESTY's Command, to be obferved and practifed by the Cavalry Corps in general, in His MAJESTY's Service.

By Command of Field Marſhal,
His Royal Highneſs
The DUKE of YORK.

WILLIAM FAWCETT,
ADJUTANT GENERAL.

INTRODUCTION.

IT is His MAJESTY's pleasure that the use and exercise of the Sword shall in future be regularly taught at the drills of the Cavalry, as an essential part of the instruction of a horseman ; and, in order to establish uniformity of execution on a proper system, the following regulations must be strictly observed.

The first principles are to be acquired and shewn on foot, under the direction of the adjutant, until such time as the squads are in a sufficient degree of forwardness to execute their lessons on horseback, when it will become the particular duty of the riding master to instruct them in the mode by which horsemanship and the use of the sword are combined.

His

His MAJESTY's Regulations for the Formation, Movements, and Field Exercise, of the Cavalry, do not suffer the smallest alteration in the practice of this system, which is calculated to give the horseman, when acting singly, that decided advantage over an enemy, which horsemanship, and a conscious superiority in the use of his sword must always produce.

CON-

CONTENTS.

———————

PART I.

A   *Method*

TELLING

TELLING OFF in BATTALION or DIVISION.

SWORD EXERCISE COMPRISED IN SIX DIVISIONS OF MOVEMENTS, WITH THE WORDS OF COMMAND.

PART II.

PART

RULES AND REGULATIONS

SWORD EXERCISE.

PART I.

THESE Regulations for the management of the Sword are laid down under the heads of OF-FENSIVE and DEFENSIVE, whether with refpect to Cavalry or Infantry; the whole being comprifed in the following Movements:

I. OFFENSIVE, fix Cuts.

II. DEFENSIVE againft *Cavalry*, eight Guards.

III. The POINT, as applied generally.

IV. The CUT and GUARD againft *Infantry*.

B   I. CUTS.

I. CUTS.

THERE are only fix ways of directing the edge of the blade; therefore the different parts of the body, which may be expofed by the unfkilfulnefs of a fwordfman, are not to be (erroneoufly) conceived as admitting of fo many diftinct Cuts. The action of the wrift and fhoulder alone directs the blade; and they admit but of fix movements, from which every cut is derived, wherever may be its particular application to the body. Of the fix cuts, four are made in diagonal directions, and two horizontally: the whole are equally applicable againft cavalry, and may be directed on either fide of the horfe, but their application muft depend on the openings given by the adverfary, and be regulated by judgment, and experience in the ufe of the weapon.

To make a Cut with effect, and at the fame time without expofing the perfon, there are two points which principally demand attention. The firft is, to acquire a facility in giving motion to the arm by means of the wrift and fhoulder without bending the elbow; for in bending the elbow, the fword-arm is expofed; a circumftance of which the opponent will ever be ready to take his advantage, as a cut in that quarter may be made with the greateft fecurity; and if it be well directed, with the moft fatal effect, as it at once decides the iffue of the conteft. The Cuts III. and IV. are particularly calculated to apply againft the wrift.

The

The next object is to attain a correctnefs in applying the edge in the direction of the blade, otherwife
it will turn in the hand; and as in that cafe the flat
part muft receive the whole force of the blow, it will
in all likelihood be fhivered to pieces.

From want of habit in the exercife of the wrift in
the common occupations of life, the weight of the
fword will at firft be found extremely irkfome. The
action of the arm bears no comparifon with that
quicknefs of which the wrift is fufceptible; for the
motions of the arm are fo wide and circuitous, that
they are eafily counteracted; from which, in a clear
point of view, the ftricteft perfeverance will be found
neceffary in order to attain perfection in the firft leffons; which are merely confined to acquiring a fup-
plenefs in the wrift and fhoulder; as without this in-
difpenfible requifite, no perfon can become a good
fwordfman.

II. GUARDS.

OF the eight Guards againft cavalry, five are for
the protection of the rider and his horfe in front, and
three for the purpofe of covering them, when under
the neceffity of retiring.

The principal pofition is diftinguifhed from the reft
by the term *Guard*, and the remaining feven by that

of

of *Protect.* The *Guard* covers the head, fhoulders, and fword-arm, from the cuts I. and II. as likewife from thofe of III. and IV. requiring, however, in the latter, a trifling inclination of the arm downwards : It is not only a pofition which affords greater fecurity than any other, but it is of fuch a nature as to render all the movements neceffary to be made from it, eafy and of quick execution.

There are two other pofitions for the defence of the horfeman in front ; namely, the *Left* and *Right Protect.* They confift fimply in moving the fword-arm to the left and right of the bridle-hand. Thefe guards are calculated to give protection equally againft the thruft, as againft the cuts V. and VI; and either in making or receiving a charge, where the compactnefs of the body of cavalry does not admit of ufing the edge of the fabre, without danger to your own line. They are alfo well adapted in a moment of general confufion (which always takes place in the fhock of two conflicting bodies) to afford a great degree of fecurity, as by a quick tranfverfe of the fword-arm, three or four times repeated from left to right, the blade can fcarcely fail to meet whatever may be pointed in that direction, before it can reach the body.

The pofition generally known by the term *Hanging Guard*, protects the horfe's head on the *near* fide; and on the *off* fide, it is covered by a guard very much refembling the *Right Protect.*

The

The firſt of the three retiring guards is for the protection of the bridle-arm, and left ſide to the rear; the ſecond for that of the right arm and ſhoulder: the laſt, which is the *St. George*, concludes the eight Guards, and is intended for the protection of the back of the head. The Guards to the rear are equally ſimple and efficacious with thoſe laid down for protection in front; but the mode of carrying them into effect differs from the general principles of this ſyſtem, as will appear from the drill exerciſe. Comparatively with the great variety of movements theſe Guards are calculated to meet, they are but few in number, and therefore more to be relied on, than when the defence depends on various circumvolutions of the blade, which in the firſt place, cannot be performed within ſo ſhort a time; and, in the ſecond, must ever be rendered more uncertain, from the difficulty of execution,

―――――――――

III. *The* POINT.

THE *thruſt* has only one mode of execution, whether applied to cavalry, or infantry : but a greater degree of caution is required in its application againſt cavalry than againſt infantry ; for if the *point* is parried, the adverſary's blade gets within your guard, which is not to be recovered again in time, as with a ſmall ſword ; the weapon being too heavy to be managed with the requiſite degree of quickneſs; for which reaſon the point ſhould ſeldom or never be

B 3 given

given in the attack, but be principally confined to the purfuit, when it can be applied with effect and without rifk.

The cafe is different in acting againft infantry, as the perfons againft whom you then direct your *point* are fo much below your own level, that the weight of your fword is not felt; confequently it is managed with greater facility than with an extended arm carried above the level of the fhoulder. Therefore, in many inftances, againft infantry, the point may be ufed with as much effect as the edge, and with the fame degree of fecurity.

IV. *The* CUT *and* GUARD *against* INFANTRY.

IN that part of the fword exercife which relates folely to its application againft infantry, there are three movements, the *point*, the *parry*, and the *cut*. The execution of the two latter movements differs from the mode laid down in the general rules for practice. This difference is occafioned by the relative fituation of the contending parties.

A perfon on horfeback is elevated fo much above thofe acting on foot, that it is neceffary for him to bend his elbow, in order to take a fweep to give his cut with effect: and this may be fecurely done, as the fword-arm is not expofed in the conteft. Only the

the four diagonal cuts can be applied againſt infantry: Cuts I. and IV. are made on the near ſide, and
II. and III. on the off-ſide of the horſe. The thruſt
of a bayonet is parried, whether made on the near,
or off-ſide, by forcing it backward or forward, as
circumſtances may direct; only it is to be obſerved,
that the parry is made with the back of the blade,
inſtead of expoſing the edge.

DRILL

DRILL ON FOOT.

THAT a recruit may be more readily brought to comprehend the intention and object of the different directions in which he will be required to carry his blade, and at the fame time in order to enable the drill officer to judge how far the motions are accurately executed; the recruit muft be placed facing a wall, at the diftance of fix feet, but not fo as to touch it with his fword when drawn.

Upon the wall, immediately in front of his pofition, defcribe a circle of two feet diameter, and full four feet from the ground, then draw two lines, which will divide the circle into four parts, each line being drawn diagonally; then a third line forming an horizontal diameter: on the different points of thofe lines place the figures 1, 2, 3, 4, 5, 6, as reprefented in *Plate* I. *fig.* 1.

This will ferve to convey the idea of that fpace, which an antagonift would occupy in point of height, and the recruit is to direct all his movements to it, upon that fuppofition; the figures denoting the fix diftinct cuts of the fabre, which are to be applied in that given fpace.

His pofition muft be erect, with his body fquare to the front, his head kept up, and eyes directed to the
object

Plate 1.

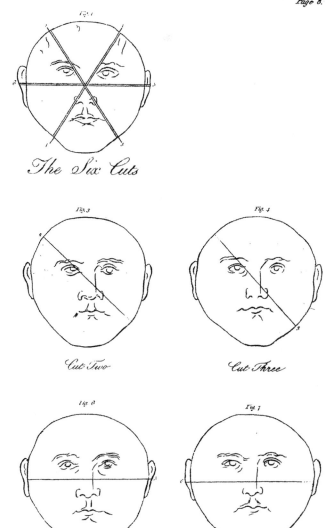

The Six Cuts

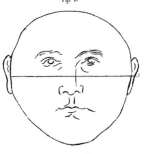

Cut One

Cut Two

Cut Three

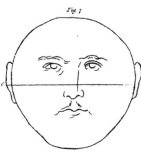

Cut Four

Cut Five

Cut Six

object before him. His heels two inches afunder, and his arms hanging without conftraint, keeping the points of his elbows back, his right hand flat on his thigh, his thumb to be on a line with the feam of his breeches; the left hand in the fame manner, with his fingers on the fcabbard to keep his fword fteady, and in readinefs to be drawn.

SWORD-KNOTS.

NO fword muft be made ufe of without having a fword-knot attached to it. It enables a perfon inftantly to recover his weapon, if forced from his grafp; and in drills, prevents accidents which are liable to occur by the fword efcaping from the hand, when not reftrained.

The fword-knot is to be made of leather, not too thick; but capable of fhaping itfelf to the wrift; yet it is not intended ever to confine the action of the wrift, which it would do if drawn tight; but it is to be of fuch a length as to admit of the fword-hilt fhifting in the hand, which is neceffary in giving point, and indeed in almoft every movement in the exercife of the fword.

In whatever form the fword-knot may be worn, it is always to be loofened the moment a dragoon becomes mounted, in order to its being in readinefs for ufe, whenever fwords are required to be drawn.

DRAW-

DRAWING *of* SWORDS.

THE fword will be drawn, and brought to the pofition in which it is to be *carried,* in three Motions.

Words of Command.

Draw fwords.

Motions.

1. Upon the word *fwords* being uttered, direct the eyes to the fword-hilt, bringing the right hand with a fharp action acrofs the body and over the bridle arm to the fword-knot, placing it upon the wrift, and giving the hand a couple of turns in-wards, in order to make it faft, at the fame time feize the hilt, and wait in this pofition for the fecond motion, which will be made by the fleugel man on the right, the back of the hand is to be to the rear.

2. Draw the fword from the fcabbard with a full extended arm, at the fame time fink the hand till the hilt of the fword is immediately under the chin, with the blade perpendicular, and the back of the hand out-wards.

3. Bring

Plate 4   Page 20.

Carry Swords

Plate 2

Slope Swords.

Words of Command.

Motions.

3.

Bring the hilt down to be in a line with the bridle-hand, the elbow near the body, the blade perpendicular, and the wrift in a fmall degree rounded, which turns the edge inwards in the direction of the horfe's left ear.

SLOPING *of* SWORDS.

Slope Swords.

KEEP the fword-arm in the exact pofition, pointed out for the carrying of fwords; but diftend the fecond, third and fourth fingers from the gripe of the fword, in order that the back of the blade may meet the hollow of the right fhoulder, where it is to be fupported with the edge directed to the front.

When in this pofition, the fword will be kept fteady, and is to be without motion, at whatever pace the horfe may be moving.

RETURN-

RETURNING *of* SWORDS.

THE fword is always to be returned from the carried pofition, and not from the floped. This is likewife executed in three motions, dreffing by the right.

Return Swords. 1. Carry the fword-hilt to the hollow of the left fhoulder, having the back of the hand outwards, and the blade perpendicular, without paufing. Drop the blade (but not the hand) to the rear clofe by the left fhoulder, directing the eyes to the fcabbard,* in which the blade is immediately to be placed and returned until the *hand* and *elbow* become in a line with each other, fquare acrofs the body, and keeping the back of the hand directed to the rear.

2. Thruft the fword home into the fcabbard, and loofen inftantly the fword-knot from the

---

* By resting the blade upon the bridle arm, the point will easily meet the scabbard.

wrift,

Plate 4.

Page 13

Prepare to Guard

Words of
Command.

Motions. wrift, keeping the hand upon
the hilt.

On the motion from the fleugel man, carry the right hand
from the hilt with a fmart action to the off fide.

PREPARE *to* GUARD.

THIS is performed in one motion, and done by
bringing the extremity of the fword-hilt up to the pit
of the ftomach, with the back of the hand outwards :
the flat of the blade to the face, and carried perpen-
dicularly. At the fame inftant the bridle-hand muft
crofs the body in a fimilar direction, and immediately
under the fword-hand, keeping the nails inwards and
hand clofed.

Let it be obferved throughout the *drill* exercife,
that each cut ends with bringing the fword back to
its pofition in the *guard*, from which the recruit
without waiting for any previous word from the drill
officer, will come immediately down to the *prepare to
guard*. This is to be continued as long as the motions are executed by a repetition of numbers.

It is when in this laft pofition, that the drill officer
will give his principal inftructions on the mode of
executing the movements following. It will eafe the

ordfword-arm, that requires fuch relief; at the fame time the conftantly carrying out the arm to the *guard*, previous to every cut during this part of the exercife, will ftrengthen the elbow, and accuftom the recruit to take a correct pofition.

GUARD.

FROM the motion to *prepare to guard*, the *guard* is done at once, by darting the fword-hand forward with the fame force, as in making a blow directed to the left ear of the opponent. This will caufe the back of the blade to be towards the face; the edge of the fword fhould be turned in a trifling degree down, in order that the fide-iron of the hilt may protect the wrift and under part of the arm. The fword to be kept nearly in an horizontal pofition acrofs the face, the point carried rather above the level of the mounting, and in an exact parallel to the front.*

---

* It being impossible to hold a guard in the horizontal position, which will protect against both the under and upper cuts, there is a necessity of giving a decided protection from one or other, that the hand and eye may be relieved from the wavering and uncertainty which would be the result of choosing a medium: in this the lower part of the arm being secure, the attention is chiefly directed to ward cut I. and II. an attempt to make which is easily perceived, and obviated by turning up the side-iron by a motion of the wrist.

The

Guard.

T Grey drawn
6th L.t Drags. Del.

Engraved by A.C. Tule

Plate 6

Page 15

A Blade Mounted with a Stirrup Hilt.

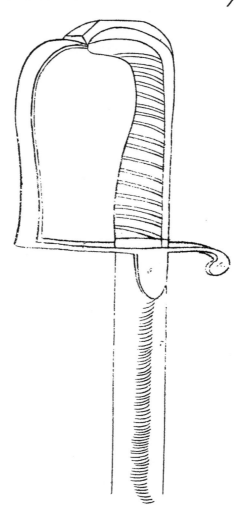

1. The Head of the Back Plate
2. The Back Plate
3. Side Iron
4. Foot of the Stirrup Iron
5. The Ear
6. The Grip
7. The outward Bord

The fight to be directed towards the antagonist, between the ear of the fword and the blade; the pofition of the blade is not to be altered for that purpofe, but the edge invariably kept down as before directed; notwithftanding it has the effect of narrowing the focus, it occafions no impediment to the fight.

In this pofition the arm should be diftended to the utmoft, and of courfe the hand above the level of the fhoulder :* the bridle-hand always remains acrofs the body, in the pofition of holding a bridle, except when the fwords are floped.

In the *guard* the greateft attention muft be paid to the correct pofition of the *hand*, which muft always be directed to the left ear of the antagonift,

* From this guard nearly every movement, offensive or defensive, can be made with rapidity and force, as the point being carried rather higher than the wrist, occasions a facility of execution in the commencement of a cut. It will therefore be found preferable to the hanging guard for a horseman; for although the hanging guard may appear to afford a greater security against the first cut of an antagonist, yet it confines those who adopt it, either to give point in the attack, or to remain almost entirely on the defensive, at least till the adversary's blow has been received, or to make cut IV. which is the weakest, and except it can be directed at the elbow, the least eligible. None of the other cuts can be made without first bringing the blade up to the position here stiled the *guard;* and the time thus lost in the motion, from the weight of the sabre, and difficulty of raising the point, when so much below the wrist, induce a preference to be given to this guard, which is a central one, from which every requisite movement may be easily effected: and from which the hanging guard may, if necessary, be taken with the greatest celerity by dropping the point.

not-

notwithftanding any change of pofition on his part.
From a guard correctly taken there is no rifque in
attacking, becaufe the fword hilt is immediately oppofed to the antagonift's retort : but when a cut originates from a falfe pofition, the head by the firft motion becomes expofed.

In oppofing cavalry the arm becomes a pivot, round
which the wrift wheels the fword independent of any
other action but what may be derived from the fhoulder : *care muft therefore be taken, neither to incline
the hand to the right or left of the given pofition, nor
to fink it below the level of the antagonift's left ear;
but above all, not to bend the elbow :* thefe are faults
which beginners are extremely apt to commit, and
which expofe the fword arm to be completely difabled.
The attention cannot be too often recalled to thefe
moft effential points in the fcience; the ftrict obfervance of which chiefly conftitutes the excellence of
the fyftem.

CUTS.

WE now come to the firft Cut, in performing
which the blade takes four diftinct pofitions, which,
when perfectly executed, are not difcernible, as the
quicknefs of action in the wrift gives them the ap-
pearance of being only one motion : therefore to affift
the comprehenfion of beginners, it will be neceffary
in the drill to diftinguifh the changes of the blade, by
the feparate paufes of 1, 2, 3, 4.

It

It is to be remarked, that the firft motion in every cut confifts in bringing the blade back to gather a fweep, at the fame inftant placing it in the direction in which it is to be applied, and the laft motion brings the blade back to the guard. The plates (7, 8, 9, 10, 11, 12,) defcribe the exact pofition of the hand, in the different motions contained in each cut.

Words of Command.	Motions.	
Guard.		FROM the *guard*, upon the word *one*, by the fole action of the wrift, draw back the blade fo as to bring the point in a perpendicular line with the outfide of the right fhoulder, for the purpofe of making a fweep:
Cut I. *in four Motions.*	1.	taking care at the time, to turn the joints of the fingers in the fame direction the cut is to be made, which will be in a diagonal courfe, as from 1 to 4. (*Plate* I. *fig.* 2.)

The recruit is too apt to fink his hand, or draw it from the guard, upon the firft motion of the cut; attention muft therefore be paid to his hand being fteady, and always covering his

C   head

Words of Command.

Motions. head with the hilt of his fword, whatever changes of pofition his blade may take in performing the different cuts.

And it is to be confidered as an invariable rule, that the direction of the finger joints regulates the edge of the blade.

2. By a quick motion of the wrift downwards, with proper attention to direct the point to number 1, the blade will be conducted to number 4.

3. Turn the wrift inwards, dropping the point fo as to bring the blade in a diagonal line acrofs the body, with the edge outwards.

4. Bend the back of the hand inwards, bringing the flat of the blade towards the face, and carrying on the motion of the wrift, till the blade arrives at its original pofition in the guard, taking care at the fame time, that in raifing the blade, it makes a fweep inwards juft to clear the elbow of the bridle hand.

The

Cut 2.

Motion 3.

Motion 2.

Motion 1.

Motion One, brings in return the Blade
towards the left Shoulder.
Two is the 2d. Motion in returning to the Guard.
Three is the last Motion in returning to the Guard.
Four is the Guard.

The recruit having been trained to perform the above in four diftinct motions with precifion; drop the repetition of figures, and let him perform them very flowly, as one motion, and then increafe the quicknefs of execution, till the cut is correctly made, with force, carrying a proper edge, and without giving action to the elbow; obferving the fame rule in the five following cuts. It muft be conftantly a part of the drill officer's inftruction to his fquad, not to hold their fwords too tight; but to allow the hilt to play in the hand, by the fecond, third, and fourth fingers being diftended or contracted, as may be neceffary to accord with the motion of the blade; taking care invariably to hold the gripe firm with the fore-finger and thumb.

———————

Words of Command.	Motions.	
		The fecond cut is made upon the principle of the preceding one. The blade takes four diftinct pofitions, and will in the drill practice, be treated accordingly.
Guard.		
Cut II. *in four Motions.*	1.	Upon the word *one*, retire the blade acrofs the face, till the point becomes nearly perpendicular to the elbow of the bridle hand.
	2.	By the action of the wrift conduct the blade in the diagonal

C 2   line

line from two to three, (plate I.
fig. 3) obferving in the execution thereof, all the rules laid
down in the preceding leffon for
conducting the edge and finger
joints.

3.   Turn the wrift to the right,
till it has brought the back of
the hand under, the nails of the
fingers and infide feam of the
right fleeve upwards; at the fame
time keeping a firm grafp of the
fword with the fore finger and
thumb, relax the other three
fingers, which will occafion the
point to fink, and the blade to
arrive in a diagonal pofition, fimilar to the line 2 and 3, with
the edge outwards.

4.   Turn the hand to the left till
it brings the fword to its original
pofition in the *Guard*, obferving
well, that in raifing the blade, it
makes a fweep round the right
fhoulder, clear of the head.

The

Plate 5.

Motion 2.

Motion 1.

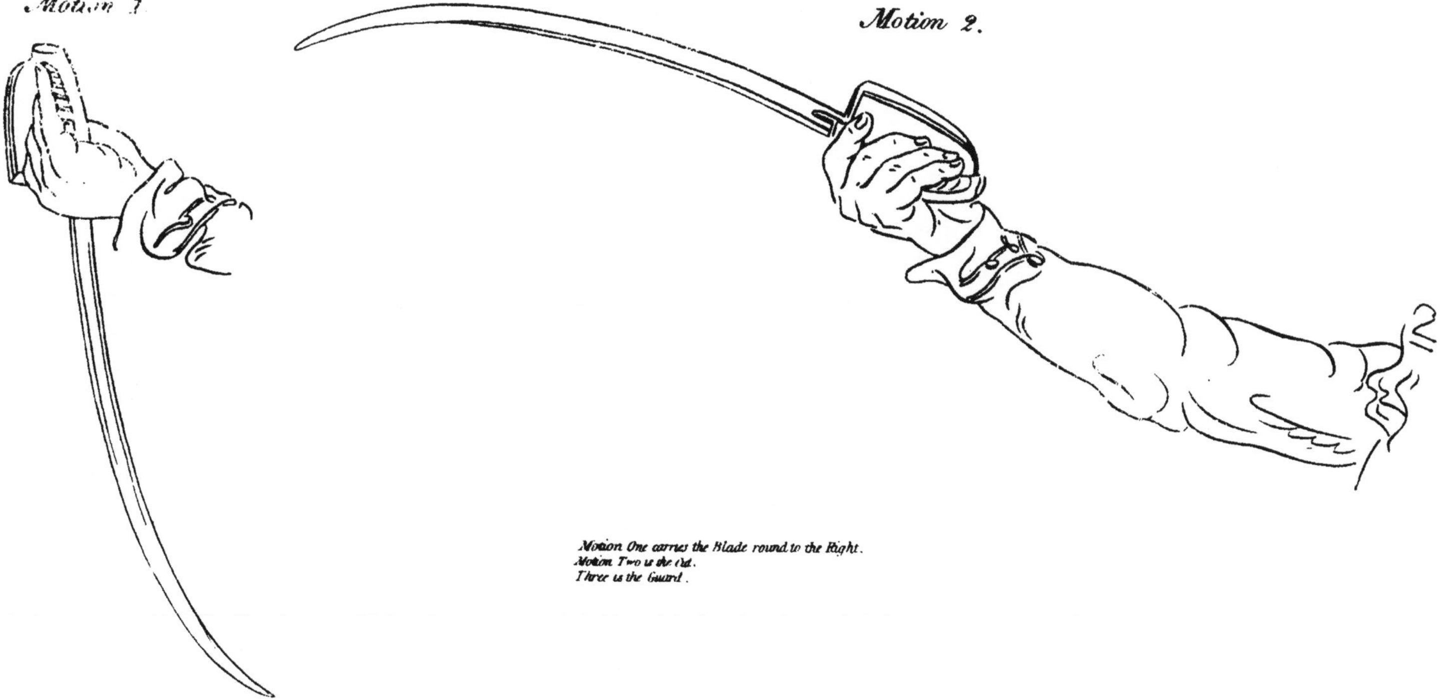

Motion One carries the Blade round to the Right.
Motion Two is the Cut.
Three is the Guard.

Words of Command.   Motions.   The next cut, *viz.* from fig. 3 to 2 (plate I. fig. 4) is made in three motions.

Guard.

Cut III. *in three Motions.*

1. Drop the point outwards to the right, by turning the wrist in that direction, and relaxing the grasp of the three fingers of the sword-hand, keeping at the same time a firm hold with the fore finger and thumb: this will bring the blade in a diagonal line, similar to the one drawn from the numbers 2 and 3, (plate I. fig. 4) with the back of the blade towards the body.

2. Conduct the point of the sword from number 3 to number 2, by bending the wrist towards the face, and pressing upon the three distended fingers, which act as a lever.

3. Come to the original guard by turning the nails under, and back of the hand up.

Too much attention cannot be paid to suppling the wrist, and the drill officer will instruct his squad in the mode of doing so,

C 3   which

Words of
Command.

Motions. which is by a repetition of the 1ſt
and 2d motions in cut III. ſeveral
times ſucceſſively without making
any pauſe on either motion,

Every leſſon ſhould begin with
ſuppling the wriſt, and which muſt
be frequently repeated during the
hours of drill: in which practice
the recruit will direct his attention to the ſteadineſs of his arm,
which is to be ſtraight, keeping
the hand above the level of the
ſhoulder.

Guard.
Cut IV. *in three*
Motions.

Cut IV. is likewiſe performed
1. in 3 motions.——By turning the
wriſt to the left, it will drop the
point in a diagonal line acroſs the
body, within three inches of the
left elbow, and with the edge of
the ſword outwards.

2. Carry the point from No. 4 to
1, (plate I. fig. 5) diagonally, by
extending the hand in a direct
line with the arm.

3. Turn the back of the hand
outwards to the right, carrying
on the motion of the blade till it
arrives at the poſition of the
guard,

Plate 10.

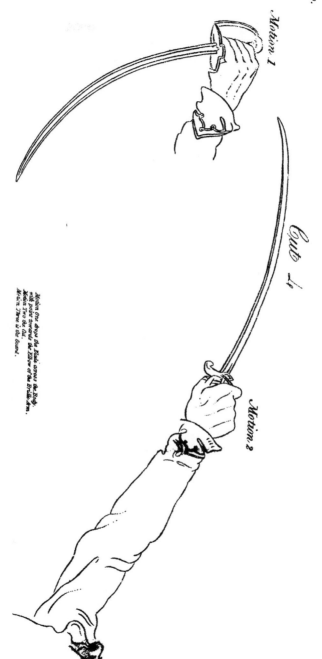

Cuts 2.

Motion 1

Motion 2

Motion One drops the Blade across the Body,
with point towards the Elbow of the Bridle Arm.
Motion Two the Cut.
Motion Three is the Guard.

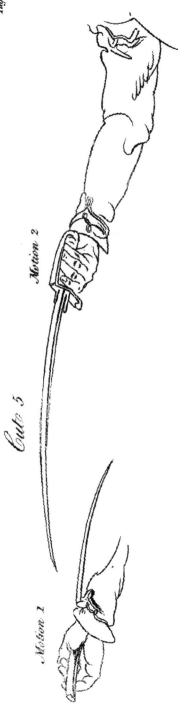

Motion 2

Cuts 5

Motion 1

Motion One is raising the Blade in a
Horizontal direction to the Right.
Motion Two is the Cut.
Motion Three the Guard.

Plate 6.

Motions. *guard,* taking care that it does not go round the head of the right ſhoulder, which would make the motion wider than neceſſary.

The cut V. is made horizontally acroſs the face from ear to ear, and executed in three motions.

Guard.
Cut V. *in three*
Motions.

1. Carry the point of the blade round to the right, with the edge directed outwards, till it reaches a little below the level of the ſword hand, and inclined towards the right ſhoulder. This is done by turning the back of the hand under, and bringing the nails up.

2. Conduct the point to No. 5, and horizontally acroſs the circle, which is done by inclining the hand inwards in the direction of the cut, without changing the poſition of the nails. (Plate I. fig. 6.)

3. Turn the wriſt into its proper poſition in the *Guard,* by bringing the back of the hand up.

Cut

| Words of Command. | Motions. | Cut VI. has the fame number of motions as the preceding one. |

Guard.

Cut VI. *in three Motions.*

1. Retire the point of the blade within a foot of the left fhoulder, finking it a little below the level of the fword hand, which is done by an inclination of the wrift towards the face.

2. Conduct the point to No. 6, and horizontally acrofs the circle to No. 5. (plate I. fig. 7,) by carrying the hand out in that direction, keeping the back of the hand ftill upwards.

3. Bring the blade in a fweep round the right fhoulder, and clear of the head to its pofition in the *Guard,* by turning the back of the hand under, and inclining it outwards, till the blade is brought nearly to the head; then turn the back of the hand to the face, and it will conduct the blade to the *Guard.—Slope Swords.*

In the foregoing motions, the beginner is apt to carry his right fhoulder too forward, and likewife to incline his head to the fword-arm. He may be allowed to do both in a fmall degree, but by no means to excefs;

Plate 12.

Cut 6.

Motion 1.

Motion 2.

Motion One consists in raising the Blade towards
the left Ear in a Horizontal direction.
Motion Two is the Cut.
Motion Three is the Guard.

cefs; and on no account fhould the recruit be permit-
ted to proceed farther in the fyftem than thefe fix cuts,
till he is perfect mafter of the preceding directions.

THE manner of performing the fix cuts fingly being
attained, the next object is to combine them, which
will occafion fome little deviation with refpect to the
mode of executing the fecond and fourth cuts, from
the principles laid down in the preceding leffons; in
which they are only treated of as they are to be applied fingly ; but the whole executed together form a
combined movement, which occafions the difference
in the mode of practice.

In cut II. the fword is not to be carried round the
right fhoulder to the pofition to guard, immediately
upon making the cut, but to be allowed to paufe upon
the third motion of the fecond cut ; in which pofition
the blade will be in the exact direction for performing
cut III. ; and where it is to remain till the word is
given for making that cut.

In cut IV. the change is in the fecond motion :
where inftead of bringing the blade to the guard in
the third movement of that cut, drop the point to the
right in the precife pofition of the firft motion in cut
V. ; and wait there for the word from the officer to
make that cut.

In combining the cuts, take care that cut II. is correctly

rectly made, it being a common fault with beginners not to carry the edge well in making that cut, in confequence of their allowing the fword hilt to turn in their hand, and not retaining that firm gripe with the fore-finger and thumb, which is indifpenfably neceffary.—Wherever this fault occurs, the recruit muft be brought back to the drill motions, and made to practife the cuts fingly till perfect.

It muft be obvious that the mode of executing the cuts two and four, according to the preceding directions, leffens the number of motions, and that each cut leads to the other, by which means, when the whole are quickly executed, the edge is carried with redoubled force, acquired by the velocity of action in the blade, in confequence of not being impeded in its courfe.*

* Whether the cuts are executed separately or collectively, that invariable rule of keeping the hand directed to the left ear of the antagonist must be adhered to, and care taken to avoid that error to which all beginners are liable, of carrying the sword hand to the right of their head previous to making cuts 1, 3, or 5, which exposes them to a return of the same cuts before any regular position of guard can be recovered. Upon the same principle they should be cautioned against inclining the hand to the left, when intending to make cuts 2, 4, 6.

It should be always remembered that the force of the stroke against a person on their own level, must be derived from the sweep of the blade, and not from the motion of the arm.

THE

Plate 13

Page 27

Left Protect

THE changes upon each cut neceffary to a combined movement having been acquired, the recruit fhould be next taught to execute all the cuts quickly and as one movement; which in the courfe of future practice will be termed the affault.

MODES *of* PARRYING.

We now arrive at the different modes of parrying to the front; they are five in number, including the one already practifed, under the denomination of the *Guard.*

The *left* and *right protect* are the two following motions, which will be performed fucceeding each other without coming to the *prepare* between the intervals of their performance.

Words of Command.

Guard.
Left Protect.

From the *guard,* carry the fword-arm fmart acrofs the body to the left*, raifing the point of the blade till it becomes perpendicular; keeping the hand above the level of the fhoulder: at the fame inftant, place the thumb on the gripe, between the back plate

* The sight should always accord with the direction of the blade, and recruits be cautioned against that absurd practice of looking one way and acting another.

and

Words of Command.

and the ear, (plate VI.) which will turn the edge of the fword to the right, and the back outwards to receive the cut; the arm to be kept as far from the body as the pofition will admit.

The elbow in this as well as in the next motion is to have no action whatever, as the whole muft proceed from the fhoulder and wrift.

Right Protect.

Without changing the direction of the blade, as held in the foregoing pofition, carry the fword-arm brifkly to the right, directing the hand to the diftance of two feet from the edge of the circle, above the level of the fhoulder —Return to the *prepare to guard.*

To preferve uniformity in the motions of *left* and *right protect*, which are both applied on the fame principle, it was neceffary to diftinguifh the immediate points to which the hand was to be directed: but when oppofed to an enemy, their application muft depend on the direction of the cuts or thrufts, which they are intended to parry.

The utmoft attention muft be paid not to oppofe the edge to the enemy's fabre when it can be avoided; but

Plate 14

Page 28

Right Protect

Plate 25

Page 60

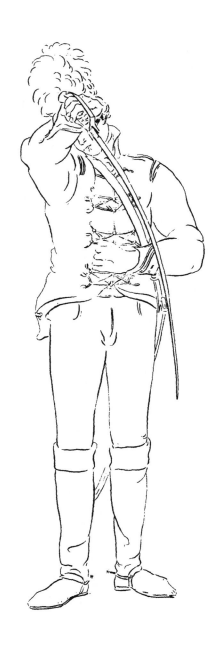

Horse near side Protect

but the bevel: which can only be done by placing the thumb between the back plate and the ear of the fword, and keeping it firm in that pofition, the arm to be properly diftended, for the purpofe of refifting the force of the blow.

The only difference neceffary to be obferved in coming to the *protect* from the *prepare*, in the place of the *guard*, is, that before the hand moves to the pofition directed, the thumb muft be fhifted to the place on the gripe already defcribed.

The two following motions are for the protection of the horfe's head, at the fame time with that of the rider.

Words of Command.

Guard.
Horfe, near fide
Protect.

Direct the point of the blade forwards to the left of the horfe's head, and in a diagonal line from the hand, which is not to droop, but to be carried a little forward, in order to afford the protection required either from cut I. or III.

The edge will be upwards in this inftance, but it muft neceffarily be expofed from the nature of the guard.

Horfe, off fide
Protect.

Raife the blade till it becomes perpendicular, carrying it at the fame inftant in a brifk motion forwards to the off ear of the horfe, and in the exact pofition of *right protect ;*

[30]

protect; not forgetting to place
the thumb in the direction therein
mentioned.—Return to the *prepare to guard.*

The different guards to the front have already been
defcribed; we therefore now proceed to the retiring
pofitions, which are performed upon a different principle, the arm being neceffarily bent to carry the
fword to the rear.

The three following guards muft be executed fucceeding each other, without coming to the *prepare*
between the intervals of their performance.

Words of
Command.

*Guard.
Bridle-arm Pro-
tect, in two
Motions.*

Motions.

1. From the pofition to guard
carry the fword in a horizontal
direction to the right; the edge
of the blade leading till it arrives
in a right line with the point of
the fhoulder.

2. Turn the back of the hand under, which will caufe the edge of
the blade to be upwards: at the
fame inftant, by bending the elbow and turning the wrift fo as to
place the palm of the hand in
front, the blade will be conducted
to the protection of the bridle-arm,
which

Plate 27   Page

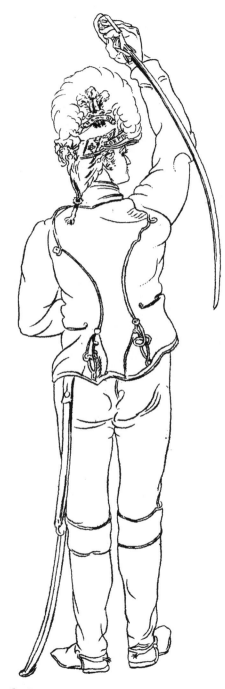

Sword Arm Protect

which pofition confifts in having the fword-hilt above the helmet, with the blade croffing the back of the head, the point of the left fhoulder, and the bridle-arm; its edge directed to the left, and turned a little upwards, in order to bring the mounting in a proper direction to protect the hand.

After protecting the bridle-arm in two motions, it is to be performed without making any paufe on the firft motion.

Sword-arm Protect. Without finking the hand from the protection of the bridle-arm, or moving the arm from its former pofition, carry the blade round the back of the head to the right, by turning the wrift till the palm of the hand arrives oppofite the helmet; the blade will then be in a diagonal line, with the point downwards directed to the right, and the edge up.

St. George. Bring the blade in a horizontal direction acrofs the top of the head, with the edge upwards and the point to the left. This is done by turning the wrift up fo

as

Words of Command. Motions. as to carry the blade round the back of the head to its pofition.

From the *St. George,* or *head protect,* come to the pofition to guard, by making that cut to the rear, which muft frequently be applicable, whenever the three re-tiring guards are fo; and which makes the full fweep of a femi-circle.

It is done upon the principle of the fixth cut, only giving edge to the rear, inftead of the front; but as the mode of executing it deviates in fome refpects from former practice, it may not be amifs to give it in detail. It is performed in two motions from the *St. George.*

To the rear Cut, in two Motions.

1. By the right, turn the body to the rear as far as poffible without moving the feet from the ground: at the fame inftant carry the blade to the rear, directing the edge as from 6 to 5, till it arrives in a right line with the arm, which will be at its full extent. The point of the blade to be kept upon a level with the fhoulder. In this pofi-

St. George.

Motions. pofition the edge will be directed
to the right with the back of
the hand upwards. Unlefs the
body turns well to the rear
when making this cut, the blade
muft be brought over the right
fhoulder in place of the left; and
fevere ftrains are liable to happen
from the arm being exerted in a
direction to which the body does
not conform.

2. Turn the back of the hand
down by a motion of the wrift
to the right, and carry the point
of the blade with a fweep over the
left fhoulder, to the proper pofition in the guard. After cutting to the rear in two motions,
execute it without paufing upon
the firft motion. Return immediately from the *guard* to the
pofition to *prepare*, without any
word from the drill officer.

GENERAL APPLICATION *of the* POINT.

The motions offenfive and defenfive beft adapted to the cavalry have now been confidered; except what relates to the point. But as that is applied upon a general principle, whether againft cavalry or infantry, it has been referved till we come to treat of the infantry part of this fyftem. It has been already mentioned, that the fword has three diftinct movements when oppofed to the infantry; arrd which can only be applied in two fituations, on the near, or off fide of the horfe. The movements confift in *giving point*, the *parry* and the *cut*.

In the drill practice, the motions in each movement will be diftinguifhed by a repetition of numbers, according to the mode already purfued. But precifion being once acquired, the recruit is to be ordered to execute them without making any unneceffary paufe upon the different motions. Let it be obferved, that the fafety and advantage in giving the point, confift in oppofing only a flank, and never a front to the antagonift, by which means the curve of a fcymitar blade covers the body, whilft the guard protects the hand.

Without

Plate 19

Page 36

Left Give Point.

P. Dury Coro.
16th L. Drag.t Del.

Words of
Command.
Motions.

Left give point,
in two motions. 1.

Without moving the feet,
turn the head round to the left,
keeping the body fquare to the
front; at the fame inftant place
the blade in a diagonal line
acrofs the body to the left, with
the edge outwards, and the
point directed as to an object
confiderably below your own
level.

This is to be done by dropping the point immediately from
the pofition *prepare to guard,*
and bending the elbow till the
knuckles of the fword-hand are
a little above the level of the
ear, and about fix inches from
the head. The forefinger and
thumb are to be diftended; the
former on the gripe, between
the ear and back plate, in a line
with the flat of the blade; and
the latter on the back plate, in a
line with the back of the blade,
by which means the extremity
of the fword hilt will fall into
the palm of the hand; which
being preft againft the three
remaining fingers will give a
firm purchafe, and the means of
applying a fteady point. The

D 2   head

Motions. head will be turned to the left, and eyes to the extremity of the blade. The recruit will wait in this pofition, for the word *two*, from the drill officer.

2. Dart the fword down in the direction in which it was held to the utmoft extent of the arm; taking care not to alter the pofition of the hand or blade, which fhould have the edge outwards, and the back of the hand up.

To the Rear, Parry, in two Motions.

1. Without changing the pofition of the hand, extend the fword-arm to the front of your ufual pofition, in order to take a fweep with the edge of the blade upwards, and kept well off from the body, upon the fuppofition of being on horfeback, fo as to prevent the fword from touching the horfe's fhoulder.

2. Bring the arm back with a quick motion to the rear, till the fword-hand arrives in a line parallel to the left ear, and fix inches from the head; at the fame inftant raife the point, till the

Plate 20

Page 11

Front Give Point.

P. Corps. Corn.
of A. 13. Drag.ᵗ Del

Words of Command.	Motions.

Words of Command.

Cut IV.

Motions. the blade becomes **perpendicular,** with the edge directed outwards to the left, and the back towards the face.

From the pofition in which the blade is left in finifhing the *parry*, bring it back to the pofition in the *guard;* carrying the edge with a good fweep outwards, taking care not to crofs with your blade parallel to your proper front, till it is brought confiderably above the level of the horfe's head; otherwife, the animal would be in danger of receiving the cut.

The following movement applies in acting againſt cavalry.

Front give point, 1.
in two Motions.

Face to the right, by turning on the heels;* at the fame inſtant retire the arm towards the ear as in giving point to the left; with this difference, that the hand is to be drawn as far back as poffible, retaining ex-

* The position of the feet being two inches asunder, the facings may be done in one motion, by turning on the heels.

actly

Words of Command.	Motions.	

actly the fame grafp of the fword The flat of the blade to be upwards, with the edge directed to the right, keeping the point horizontal with the hand, and the fword carried above the peak of the helmet. The head is to be turned to the left, in the fame direction with the point. Upon all occafions in *giving point* againft cavalry, the fword is to be carried above the peak of the helmet, and by preffing the blade againft the helmet it will be kept fteady.

2. Dart the hand in the direction of your proper front, to the full extent of the arm; turning at the fame time to the left about, keeping the blade ftill horizontal, and without changing the pofition of the hand, which ought to be with the back upwards.

Cuts V. VI. Retire the blade in its horizontal direction to the right, in doing which, bring the back of the hand under and carry the blade immediately to the cuts V. and VI. when return to the *prepare to guard,* from the laft cut,

Plate 21   Page 38

Right Give Point.

Words of
Command.

Motions. cut, bringing the body round
to the proper front.

Right give point,   1.   Turn the head to the right as
in two Motions.   much as can be done without
                          moving the body, which is to be
                          kept fquare to the front; at the
                          fame time bring the fword-hand
                          up to the ear, having in grafp
                          as before, with the back of the
                          hand up, and the edge of the
                          blade in the fame direction as in
                          making the thruft on the near
                          fide, carrying the point as much
                          to the right, as in the other in-
                          ftance, it was directed to the
                          left of your ufual front.

                      2.   Dart your fword down to the
                          full extent of the arm, without
                          changing the pofition of the
                          hand.

Rear parry, in   1.   Without changing the pofi-
two motions.   tion of the hand, carry the blade
                          towards your front to gather a
                          fweep; in doing which turn the
                          edge of the blade up, and the
                          back of the hand under. This
                          will bring the back of the blade
                          oppofite your front.

                      2.   Without changing the pofition
                          D 4   of

of the hand, by a fharp action of
the fword-arm to the rear, carry
the fword as far back as the arm
will admit of, the hand to be on
a level with the point of the
fhoulder, the blade carried perpendicular, with the edge directed towards the rear, and the
back to the front.

From the *parry*, bring the
fword to the proper pofition of
the *guard*, by carrying an edge
with a good fweep outwards,
and with the fame precaution
not to crofs parallel to the front
on account of the horfe. Return from the *guard* to the pofition of *flope fwords*.

THE movements of the fword have been confidered
upon drill principles, in which the attention was directed folely to clafs them in fuch a manner, as to lead
the recruit progreffively to the different changes of
which the blade is fufceptible, that he may acquire a
perfect execution of each feparately; the motions having not the leaft reference to what may be their pofitions when arranged under a proper fyftem of exercife.

AFTER having attained to a tolerable degree of
accuracy, the mode of executing feparately the
movements

movements already laid down, it will be proper next to proceed to perform the fword exercife by the word of command, taking the motions at the fame time from fleugel-men, according to the principle obferved in the manual exercife.

To front the wall will be no longer neceffary, as it is to be suppofed that the pofition o every cut as defcribed on the circle (to which all former practice has been applied) muft now be fully in the recollection of the recruit.

The head muft follow the direction of every motion, two fleugel-men will therefore be neceffary, one on each flank; who are to be careful to take up the time from each other, according to the change of pofition, or dreffing point from right to left.

The diftance of files will be laid down for the practice of the fword exercife in battalion and fmaller divifions.

The battalion to be told off in wings, and ranks of threes.

TELLINGS OFF *in* BATTALION *or* DIVISION.

Words of Command.

Rear rank take diftance for fword exercife.

THE right and left hand men of the rear rank belonging to both wings, will retreat nine paces, dreffing by the right.

March.

Words of Command.

March.

The rear rank falls back and dreffes by the pivots ; the fleugel-men will at the fame time take their diftances to the front.

From the centre of the battalion open your files. March. The men of the right wing inftantly open out, placing their bridle hands in the hollow of the left fide, fo as to barely touch with their elbows their left hand files.

The left wing will open out, and upon the fame principle infure the diftance of files, by means of the right arms.

The rear rank to do the fame.

The arms to be kept up, till brought down by a motion from the right fleugel-man.

Great attention from the drill officer is requifite, in order to obferve that the proper diftances of files are taken, to prevent unpleafant accidents which may otherwife occur, and on this account the arm fhould be kept bent, till he has feen that the diftances are correctly obferved.

Upon

Prepare to perform fword exercife.

Upon thefe words of command, the right fub-divifion of each wing will give the diftances of files in the manner following.

The right hand man of ranks by threes ftands faft, the centre man takes three paces to the rear of the right hand file and covers him.

The left-hand man of the divifion retreats fix paces and covers the two preceding file of his divifion.

The doubling files are all to ftep off with the right feet, the rear rank does the fame, covering the front rank files.

The right-hand files of all the divifions ftand faft: the left and centre men taking their diftances as before directed: *officers and non-commiffioned officers to the rear, except fuch as are told off in ranks of threes.

---

* The non-commissioned officers to be one horse's length to the rear, covering a file, the officers at the distance of two horses length.

By

By this movement the battalion will become fix deep.

As an aukward man may occasion a ferious accident, by not exactly covering his file, it will be moft fafe to prove their diftances, which is to be done as follows.

To the right prove diftance of files.

*Taking the motions from the fleugel-man, every man will point his fword to the right at the full extent of his arm, keeping the blade horizontal, and in a line with the fhoulder; the edge directed the fame way, and the hilt held in the precife manner, as when giving point in that direction. The body to be kept fquare to the front, with the head turned to the right.

When each file has had time to fee whether he has his proper diftance, and corrected it where required, (which muft be inftantly done with a fteady eye and prompt decifion) they will

---

* The right-hand men of the line remain with their swords sloped, having no distance to prove.

be

Words of Command.

be directed to return to the position of *slope swords*.

On this word of command, the swords are to be brought down together to the position directed, in doing which the point is not to be dropped.

To the front, prove distance of files.

This is to be done, in every respect according to the rules laid down for giving point to the right; carrying the sword forward with caution, so as not to wound the file in front, should the distance not have been preserved. The front rank remains with swords sloped, upon the principle laid down for the files on the flanks on the line.

Slope Swords.

The swords to return to the *slope,* the body kept square to the front.

SWORD

SWORD EXERCISE *on* FOOT.

THE fword exercife confifts of the motions already defcribed, arranged in fix diftinct claffes of offenfive and defenfive movements, with reference to their application in thofe fituations which are moft likely to occur on actual fervice.

Explanatory notes of the principles of application comprifed in each movement will be given, and likewife further inftructions as to the mode of executing the different motions, which being now combined with others, vary in fome refpects from the directions that have been laid down for performing them fingly. As the fword exercife, when acquired, is to be executed by one word of command to each divifion of movements, the memory muft be affifted as much as poffible in order to enable every perfon to recollect the motions, as they fucceed each other; for which purpofe the following leading points fhould be obferved.

Each divifion of movements commences with coming to the *prepare to guard*, from the pofition of *flope fwords*, and is fucceeded by the *guard*.

The pofition *prepare to guard* always fucceeds the laft motion of the fix cuts, to which pofition the fword is immediately to be brought, without paufing in the leaft on the laft motion of the preceding movement.
The

The point is always given from the pofition to *prepare* without firſt coming to the *guard*, excepting in the laſt divifion of movements; and notwithſtanding that in the other five divifions it may be given to the Right and Left, yet between each thruſt come to the *prepare*, as it is to originate from that pofition. The *left* and *right protect* are likewife made from the *prepare to guard*.

Each movement invariably concludes with the motions *prepare to guard,* the *guard,* and *ſloping* of fwords.

The memory will therefore have to charge itſelf only with the particular motions which belong to each of the ſix divifions of movements. This will be rendered perfectly clear by the words of command which characterize the movements being diſtinguiſhed by numbers.

———————

WORDS

WORDS *of* COMMAND.

Perform Sword Exercife by Word of Command.

Firft Divifion of Movements.

		From which Fleugelman the Motion is to be taken.
	Prepare to guard.	Right.
	Guard.	Right.
No. 1.	*Affault.*	Right.
No. 2.	*Left protect.*	Right.
No. 3.	*Right protect.*	Left.
No. 4.	*Prepare to guard.*	Right.
No. 5.	*Front give point.*	Right.
	*Prepare to guard.	Right.
	Guard.	Right.
	Slope fwords.	Right.

It is to be an invariable rule to return to the *prepare to guard,* upon the laft motion of the fixth cut.

It is alfo to be recollected that the head turns and remains fixt in the direction to which the motion points.

* Drop the point, and bring it with a sweep round the left elbow to the *prepare to guard.*

The

The motions throughout the exercife are to be performed fharp and correctly, paying ftrict attention to
the dreffing points.

In this firft divifion, there are only five motions
which are not conformable to the general rule already
ftated.

The points of dreffing given oppofite the words of
command, fhew from which fleugelman the particular
motions are to be taken; and it is to be confidered as
matter of courfe, that the head and eyes follow the
direction of each motion.

Explanation of the Firft Divifion of Movements.

The *affault* reprefents the charge, where the fix Cuts
are directed indifcriminately to the *right* and *left*.

The *protects* are againft the returning cuts of the
enemy.

The *point* is given on a fuppofition of the enemy's
retiring.

E   WORDS

WORDS of COMMAND.

Second Division of Movements.

		Fleugelman.
	Prepare to Guard.	Right.
	Guard.	Right.
No. 1.	*Assault.*	Right.
No. 2.	*Guard.*	Right.
No. 3.	*Bridle-arm protect.*	Right.
No. 4.	*Sword-arm protect.*	Left.
No. 5.	*St. George.*	Right.
*No. 6.	*Rear cut.*	Right.
	Guard.	Right.
	Slope Swords.	Right.

Explanation of the Second Division of Movements.

The *assault* reprefents the charge.

Guarding the *Bridle-arm* denotes being obliged to
retreat, and as the purfuer will generally attack the
near fide, it is the fafeft pofition to receive him in, as
it not only covers the arm, but, as the enemy paffes,

---

* Upon the last motion of the cut, return to the *prepare to guard.*

carry

carry the blade forwards, by moving the hand in that direction, it will alfo give protection to the whole of the near fide.

The fword-arm is fuppofed to be attacked by a fecond purfuer, the moment the firft is gone paft, who makes his advance on the off fide, in confequence of feeing the attack on the near defeated.

In the defence of the fword-arm the head and fhoulders are expofed, to which an offenfive movement is made, and parried by coming to the pofition *St. George:* the retreat is completed by giving cut **VI.** to the rear.

WORDS *of* COMMAND.

Third Divifion of Movements.

		Fleugelman.
	Prepare to guard.	Right.
	Guard.	Right.
No. 1.	*Affault.*	Right.
No. 2.	*Guard.*	Right.
No. 3.	*Horfe's near fide protect.*	Right.
No. 4.	*Horfe's off fide protect.*	Left.
*No. 5.	*Cuts I. II. I.*	Right.

* Upon the last motion in cut I. come to the *Prepare to guard,* by dropping your point as before directed.

E 2

No. 6.

Fleugelman.

No. 6.	*Left Protect.*	Right.
No. 7.	*Right Protect.*	Left.
No. 8.	*Prepare to guard.*	Right.
No. 9.	*Front give point.*	Right.
*No. 10.	*Cut I.*	Left.
	Guard.	Right.
	Slope fwords.	Right.

* Return to the *prepare to guard.*

Explanation of the Third Divifion of Movements.

The *affault* is the charge.

The horfe's head is attacked and protected.

By the antagonift's fecond cut at the horfe, he expofes his own head, which opening is taken advantage of in making the cuts I. II. I. and which he parries by coming to the *left* and *right protect*, and returns the point with cut I.

WORDS

WORDS of COMMAND.

*Fourth Divifion of Movements.

	Fleugelman.
Prepare to guard.	Right.
Guard.	Right.
† No. 1. *On your right to the front parry*	Right.

* As this part of the subject relates to acting against infantry, attention must be paid to the principles given in the drill lessons, for the application both of the point and edge of the sabre.

† Parry the bayonet in the same manner to the front, as in the drill lessons was practised to the rear. And upon the word of command being given, retire the sword-arm as far to the rear as possible, the edge of the blade leading in a horizontal direction, and in a line with the shoulder; when arrived at the extent of the arm, the action of the wrist is to carry on the motion of the blade till it becomes perpendicular, with the point upwards and back of the blade to the front. These motions must be executed with spirit. The Fleugelman will pause a little in this position, and then make his parry to the front, in completing which he recovers his sword over the left shoulder, to be in readiness for cuts II. and I. In bringing his blade from the parry to its position for making his cuts, the moment it has past over the horse's head, he carries the point with a sweeh round his left to the rear; the back of the sword-hand to touch the left temple, the edge of the blade upwards, with the back resting on the shoulder, and the point sunk considerably below the level of the hand. In this position wait for the order to cut II. and I.; the former on the off, and the latter on the near side of the horse.

No. 2.

Fleugelman.

*No. 2. *Cuts II. and I.*   Right and Left.

No. 3. *Right give point.*   Right.

No. 4. *Prepare to guard.*   Right.

No. 5. *Left give point.*   Left.

†No. 6. *Cuts III. and IV.*   Left and Right.

Guard.   Right.

Slope fwords.   Right.

————————

Explanation of the Fourth Divifion of Movements.

The charge of a line of infantry in a narrow pafs occupied by them on both fides.

* In giving edge against infantry the body must be turned in the direction of the cut, and correspond with the action of the blade; and in recovering the sword from one side to the other, let it cross the head in the position described by the *St. George;* and pause a second whilst in that attitude, till the eye is supposed to have fixed on its object. From the last motion in cut I. return to the *prepare to guard.*

Cut III. is made on the off side, and IV. on the near side of the horse.

† The same directions given in the preceding note are to be followed in this instance, recollecting, that cut IV. is executed in two motions, as before pointed out in the drill practice of infantry movements, viz. The first motion is to place the blade in the precise position directed in the second movement of the left parry, and from which the cut is to be made.

The

Cut Two against Infantry.

The firſt movement is to force the bayonets off to the front on the off ſide, and applying the edge to the right and left, with the point, keeping both ſides of the enemy occupied, till the defile is ſuppoſed to be paſſed.

WORDS *of* COMMAND

*Fifth Diviſion of Movements.

	Fleugelman.
Prepare to Guard.	Right.
Guard.	Right.
†No. 1. *Left Cut I. and II.*	Left.

* This being the Defence of one horseman againſt the Attack of two, one on each side, the cuts and thrusts are to be made as much to the right and left of his front, as in the infantry practice, only the sword-arm to be kept well up, as directed for all cavalry movements.

† Carry the arm to the left, preserving the sword in the exact poſition of the guard, and make cuts I. and II.

In the third motion of cut II. the blade must be clear of the horse's head, and on the off side. The body in the same instant is to be turned to the right, bringing the blade in the *fourth motion*, up to the position of the guard in that direction. The difficulty experienced by beginners in making this cut on the near side originates from their suffering the hand to sink from the given position of the guard.

E 4   No.

Fleugelman.

*No. 2.	*Right Cut I. and II.*	Right.
No. 3.	*Left give point.*	Right.
No. 4.	*Prepare to guard.*	Left.
†No. 5.	*Right give point.*	Right.
‡No. 6.	*Cuts V. and VI.*	Left and Right.
	Guard.	Right.
	Slope fwords.	Right.

Explanation of the Fifth Divifion of Movements.

The defence of one man againft two.

The cuts applied on both fides are the offenfive movements toward each antagonift as he approaches.

The left give point, is to the enemy on the left; and the right, for the one in that direction, whom he has at bay by remaining on the longe, waiting the approach of

---

* Return to the *prepare to guard* upon the conclusion of the last motion in cut II.

† The moment the point is given, turn the edge of the blade to the front, and head to the left, keeping the arm and sword extended in a right line, in readiness to make cut V. on the near side, as soon as it is supposed the antagonist is within reach.

‡ Cut V. is made on the rear, and VI. on the off side of the horse; and upon the last motion of cut VI. come to the *prepare to guard.*

the

the other antagonift: at whom he makes cut **V.** the moment he is fuppofed to be within reach: and cut **VI.** in the oppofite direction.

WORDS *of* COMMAND.

Sixth Divifion of Movements.

		Fengelman,
	Prepare to guard.	Right.
	Guard.	Right.
No. 1.	*Right give point.*	Right.
*No. 2.	*Cuts I. and II.*	Right.
†No. 3.	*Left parry.*	Left.
‡No. 4.	*Left protect.*	Left.

---

* Cuts I. and II. are made on the off side.

† Left parry is done in two motions. The first by bringing the sword-hand into the hollow of the left shoulder, upon the last motion in cut II. keeping the back of the hand outwards, and the point perpendicular. Second motion, drop the point of the blade as much to the rear of the near side as possible, making the circle by bringing it round to the front in the same position.

‡ As the defence is made to an attack on the near side, in pursuit, the left protect must be carried as much to the left as the arm will permit; and the right protect, not to the off side, as in an attack to the front, but in the direction of the horse's left ear.

No.

		Fleugelman.
No. 5.	*Right protect.*	Left.
No. 6.	*Front give point.*	Left.
	Prepare to guard.	Left.
	Guard.	Right.
	Slope swords.	Right.

Explanation of the Sixth Division of Movements.

The modes of making an attack on the near fide of a retiring enemy, with the means of defeating it, fuppofing it to be done in fpeed.

Offenfive. { Give point to the right, and make cuts I. and II. by which time the enemy is fuppofed to have rode paft.

Defenfive. { Receive the enemy with the fword-hand in the hollow of the left fhoulder, ready either to protect or parry : as he makes his thruft, drop your blade outwards ; it will carry off his point. Cuts I. and II. are protected by the left and right protect ; and by checking your horfe, let your opponent pafs, and inftantly give him the point.

As foon as each divifion of movements is correctly executed by word of command ; it muft then be performed

formed by only one word, fpecifying the particular divifion of movements.

The motions are all to be taken from the fleugelman, without waiting for any other command than the one already mentioned.

———

AFTER the exercife is performed, it will be neceffary to bring the battalion into its proper formation, which may thus be done.

Words of Command.

Front form line.
March. | Upon which the centre and left-hand men of divifions, run up, and drefs by the pivot.

Rear rank clofe to the front.
March. | To be done according to the cuftom of the fervice.

To the center, clofe your files.
March. | This is executed with the fide ftep.

———

PART

PART II.

DRILL on HORSEBACK.

TO become a perfect cavalry fwordfman, horfeman-
fhip is indifpenfably neceffary, and without it,
very little benefit can be derived from the fcience.
Good riding does not confift in urging a horfe forward with precipitation and checking him with vio-
lence, but a dragoon and his horfe fhould be fo
formed to each other as to act as one body : for which
purpofe the rider fhould make himfelf acquainted
with the temper and powers of the animal, fo that by
a judicious management, the horfe may be rendered
docile, and execute readily whatever may be expected
of him.

Great patience will be required in training the
horfes to quit the ranks readily, if they have been
accuftomed only to act in fquadron. And it is alone
by temper and perfeverance, not by feverity, that vice
is to be conquered, and thofe tricks furmounted
which in horfes generally originate in timidity.

Before the fword exercife is attempted to be performed on horfeback, it will be neceffary to render
the

the horfes fteady, by accuftoming them to the fight of the fabre; which is eafily effected, by frequently making the cuts V. and VI. to the front, and dropping the blade both on the near and off fide, as is done in faluting. The horfe fhould never be ftruck with the fword, as it will render him unfteady, and his apprehenfion afterwards will never allow him to face the weapon, which will have the effect of placing his rider on the defenfive whenever attacked.

The regiment being mounted, and the fwords drawn for the purpofe of performing the fword exercife, the diftance of ranks and files is to be taken as follows.

DISTANCE *of* RANKS *on* HORSEBACK.

Words of Command.

Rear rank rein back for fword exercife. The diftance on the wings to be marked as directed in the foot practice.

March. The rear rank reins back 4 horfes' lengths, and dreffes by the pivots.

Prepare to perform fword exercife. The right fubdivifion of each wing, to mark the diftance of files in the manner directed for the foot practice; allowing the diftance

diftance of the third of a horfe's length between head and croup.

March. The center and left files rein back, till claar of the ftanding flank, when they will file to the right, and drefs by the pivots, taking care to cover correctly, by placing their horfes fquare to the front.

The diftance of files is to be proved, as executed on foot.

SWORD EXERCISE *when* MOUNTED.

Perform fword exercife in fix divifions of movements, by fleugelman.
Firft divifion.

In completing each divifion of movements, the line will return to the pofition of flope fwords, when they will remain feated fteady, dreffing to the right, and without the leaft motion whatever.

After a paufe of two feconds, the commanding officer will repeat the next word of command.
In

In the like manner he muft repeat his commands through the remaining four divifions, which are comprifed in the fword exercife.

The reins muft be held very fhort, fo as to enable the rider by the leaft action of the bridle-hand, to regulate the motion of his horfe's head, in order to prevent the blade from being obftructed in its courfe: and that the tightnefs of the reins may not occafion any reining back, or impatience in the animal; take care to eafe him by carrying the hand fufficiently forward for that purpofe; at the fame time feel his mouth without bearing a dead weight in that direction.

THE exercife muft at firft be performed flow, till great correctnefs of execution in every motion is attained.

In each cut, made either to the right or left of the front, the bridle-hand is to feel the horfe's mouth to the oppofite direction, in order to prevent the poffibility of danger to the animal. If this is not done

with

with judgment, the horfe will become unfteady. The flighteft inclination of the hand is fufficient for the purpofe required, if the reins are properly held. There is no danger whatever of wounding the horfe, provided the edge of the blade is kept outwards agreeable to the drill inftructions: or of its being impeded in moving either to the front or rear, if attention is paid not to crofs parallel to your front, till the point of the fword is brought above the level of the fhoulder. Too much attention cannot be paid to thefe particulars, as on their obfervance the fafety of the animal and dexterity in the exercife of the fabre in a great meafure depend. The pofitions of *carry* and *flope fwords* are the fame when on horfeback, as executed on foot.

In performing the fix divifions of movements, it is to be obferved as an invariable rule in coming to the *guard*, to rife in a fmall degree in the ftirrup, but *not clear* of the faddle, and to return to the ufual feat on horfeback with the motion to *flope fwords.*

The affault and the different guards both to the front and rear have no particular variation from the foot practice.

In the fourth divifion, whether executed in line or fpeed, the body is to be kept erect, and in either giving edge or point againft infantry, the force muft be derived from the motion of the arm, not from an inclination of the body, the balance of which fhould be preferved, otherwife the horfeman becomes expofed to the
thruft

Garde

thruft of a bayonet at the inftant his pofition renders him incapable of parrying it.

In giving point to the front, the toe of the left foot muft be *turned in* to the horfe's fide, and the heel out, otherwife it would be impoffible to bring the left fhoulder and elbow in the direction required in the firft motion, which confifts in placing them in a line with the horfe's head.

The fame rule muft be obferved in cutting to the rear. Whatever movement is made, whether applied to cavalry or infantry, *the balance of the body muft be preferved by means of the knees and thighs, without throwing the weight partially on either ftirrup;* as upon fervice, horfes are very fubject to flip through their girths, notwithftanding every poffible attention that may be paid to remedy the inconvenience; therefore, if the balance is not preferved, the faddle will turn and difmount the rider, of which many fatal examples have occurred.

SWORD DRILL *moving in* CIRCLE.

IN order to apply fkilfully in actual fervice, the different movements of the fword comprifed in this exercife, it will be abfolutely neceffary to acquire a firm feat on horfeback. For this purpofe the regiment muft be trained by the riding mafter in fquads

F   of

of eighteen or twenty men, to perform the exercife in a correct feat, when moving round a circle in a hand gallop. The precife pofition confifts in placing the foot fo far into the ftirrup, as to bring the inner part of the ball of the foot on the outer rim of the ftirrup iron.

From the hip bone downwards, the leg and thigh are to be turned round to the faddle, the knee joint nearly ftraight, the toes turned well in, and the heels funk as low as they will admit of. According to thefe inftructions, the knee and thigh will have fo firm a gripe of the faddle, that neither the lofs of a ftirrup, nor any fudden motion of the animal can fhake the rider from his pofition. The belly and cheft are to be brought forward, whilft the points of the fhoulders are preffed back, and the head carried well up. The only motion of the body below the faddle, is to be derived from the inftep, and above it from the fmall of the back. Attention muft be paid in every particular to the rules laid down for the foldier's pofition on horfeback; as omiffion in any point would prevent his ever acquiring a firm feat. Great care fhould likewife be taken that the heels are funk well down, otherwife the balance of the body, which ought to be thrown backwards, will be brought forward, when a fudden halt is liable to difplace the rider.

The length of the ftirrups will be fitted to the under part of the inner ancle bone.

As in this mode of practice there are no fleugelmen, the motions are not required to be executed fo exactly together,

together, the object being principally to attain a correctnefs of execution, and a firm pofition on horfeback.

The different movements will at firft be executed
by word of command at a walk, and the fquad is not
to be made to gallop, until they have acquired a con-
firmed feat, and execute their motions with fpirit and
precifion.

When they perform in a gallop, the pace is to be
regulated by order, and after every divifion of movements to be brought from the gallop to the trot, then
to the walk, and finally to be halted.

Attention muft be paid that the horfe leads with
the proper leg, and the practice fhould be equally directed to the left and right.

Want of exactnefs, either in the pofition of individuals or the execution of the exercife, muft be
promptly corrected ; and frequently it will be neceffary to halt them for that purpofe, in order to inftruct
feparately the perfon who may require it.

As the exercife in circle is fevere for the horfes,
much is left to the difcretion and judgment of the
drill officer, who is required to pay great attention in
this refpect, and particularly in the forming of heavy
cavalry.

The diftance of a horfe's length is to be preferved
between each file.

The

The SIX DIVISIONS *of* MOVEMENTS
Performed in Speed.

As foon as the fquad is able to perform the exercife moving in circle, let them execute the fame in fpeed upon a right line. For which purpofe draw up the fquad in rank entire at the extremity of a range of two hundred yards; the drill officer placing himfelf at the intermediate diftance, where he will be beft able to fee and correct their movements.

Only one man is to perform at the fame time: they will all execute individually the fix divifions, beginning with the firft, which they are to repeat till the fquad has rode paft as many times as may be requifite to confirm them in the perfect execution of the motions and management of the horfe. As each man concludes his divifion of movements, he is to form at the oppofite end of the range from whence he fet off, and fronting the remainder of the party.

It will frequently be found neceffary for the drill officer to ride by the fide of the perfon performing the divifion, in order to regulate the pace, which fhould never exceed three quarters fpeed, at the fame time, to correct the rider's pofition on horfeback, and infure precifion in the different movements; as on no account is the fmalleft deviation to be admitted in the mode of practice pointed out for performing the exercife in line.

RUNNING

Plate 22

Page 69

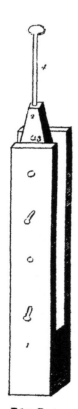

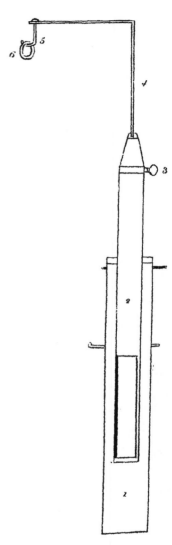

Edge Post
Viewd in Front

1 *The Body*
2 *The Slider*
3 *A Brass Screw*
4 *Willow Twig*

Ring Post
Viewd in Profile

1 *The Body*
2 *The Slider which can be fixt to any Height required*
3 *a Brass Screw*
4 *a Triangle*
5 *Hook to place the Ring on*
6 *The Ring*

RUNNING *at the* RING.

HAVING acquired a firm feat on horfeback and correctnefs in the execution of the fword exercife with the horfe in fpeed; the next qualification requifite is to attain precifion in the application of the point and the edge.

Running at the ring is adapted for the particular purpofe of training the fwordfman to carry his point with certainty to any given fpace, which muft be the refult of repeated habit and long practice.

The mode of practice confifts in giving point through a ring, which is fufpended at the degree of height which cavalry is fuppofed to occupy.

The ring is to be made of metal, and to meafure in diameter five inches, the inner circle to be four inches, and the depth one quarter. This is the largeft fize which ought to be employed, and is only adapted to beginners, who muft be progreffively led in their practice from large to fmall rings, till they are enabled to give point with tolerable degree of certainty, within the diameter of a crown piece.

In order to fufpend the ring at the height required, a machine will be neceffary, the particular conftruction of which will be exemplified in plate XXII. It will anfwer the purpofe of placing the ring in all

F 3   the

the different directions in which it can be requifite to apply the point.

This machine, which by way of diftinction will be termed the ring poft, muft be placed in a fituation where there is a tolerable even furface of feventy yards, allowing a range of fifty, or five and fifty, yards up to the ring, and fifteen beyond it, which will be more than fpace fufficient to check the moft auk-ward horfe.

In running at the ring, there are two things to be acquired; firft, extreme precifion in giving point; and fecondly, great promptitude and dexterity in bringing the horfe to the right or left about.

The perfon who is to run at the ring will place himfelf mounted at the extremity of the range, (and when giving point to the front) oppofite the ring.

His bit rein muft be drawn up fhort, keeping it firm between his fore finger and thumb, in order that he may be able to check his horfe within the fhorteft compafs poffible: he muft be feated in his faddle with his fword floped   the firft ten paces he ought to move in a trot, and then put his horfe into a canter, taking care that he leads with his off leg, at the fame time the rider will prefs on the ftirrups, by finking the heel and ftraitening the knee, and bring his fword in the pofition of *prepare to guard.* As he approaches the ring, he muft increafe his fpeed, fo as to arrive at it with confiderable rapidity; when within fifteen yards, let him bring his fword to the pofition of the guard,

and

Front Gun Point

and finally to that of giving point to the front the inftant he is within diftance to make the thruft. This he muft do, directing the point to the center of the circle, which by being carried elevated a little above the level of the hand, muft neceffarily caufe the ring to fall down to the fword mounting, provided the blade was properly directed.

The moment the point has been given come to the *fword arm protect* ;* check the horfe and bring him to the right about in order to get on the antagonift's near fide before he can bring his own horfe round ; the advantages of which manœuvre will be obvious to perfons acquainted with the principles of fkir- mifhing.

Beginners are extremely apt to divide their atten- tion in the direction of the blade, between the point and the ring, which, almoft to a certainty makes them fail in the proper aim, the fight being diftracted, between the two objects.

The mode that ought to be purfued, is to fix the attention entirely on the ring, and not to look in the leaft to the pofition of the blade, which will always follow the direction of the fight.

* In an attack of cavalry, no movement can be made without being in consequence open to a retort. It therefore must be an in- variable rule, after making an offensive movement, to come to the protection of the part exposed thereby. If in passing your antagonist, a thrust or cut is made by you on the right, come immediately after to the position of *sword-arm protect*, and look well to the rear in that direction. If the movement is made to the left, then come to the protection of the bridle-arm.

F 4

Whether

Whether in encountering your enemy, or in pur-
fuing him, obferve as an invariable rule, never to
allow your horfe to be in a line parallel with his at
the inftant of attack, as it would expofe your horfe's
head unneceffarily. Therefore in receiving your
antagonift on the off fide, incline your horfe to the
left when within the diftance of a couple of yards of
each other, in order that your fword-arm may meet
him in a direct line. Whereas moving parallel, your
horfe's head would have been the firft point within
reach of his fabre. Upon the fame principle, when
in purfuit, turn your horfe in the oppofite direction
to that in which you come up with your enemy. It
will be neceffary to attend to the fame mode of ad-
vancing, when running at the ring, or in giving edge.

In giving point to the left, come with your horfe to
the left about, and to the right about when giving to
the right or front.

The rules laid down for running at the ring in one
direction, hold good with refpect to the others, and
the practice confifts in giving point againft cavalry to
the front, on the off and near fides. Likewife againft
infantry, as practifed at the foot drill, with this difference, that in place of the ring, a 'ball formed of
canvas or cloth, and ftuffed with hay, muft be placed
at the height required for foot practice.

APPLI-

APPLICATION *of the* EDGE.

PRECISION in the application of the edge is as neceffary in acting againft cavalry or infantry, as of the point. It therefore is requifite to acquire correctnefs of execution by frequent practice, which in order to preferve the fwords, muft be addreffed to fubftances of the leaft refiftance. It will therefore be neceffary to eftablifh willow fticks lately cut, on the top of which place a turnip, or any other fubftance of as little refiftance, and againft which the edge of the fword may be directed.

It being impoffible to furnifh in fufficient quantities, willows of the height and fize that are neceffary, a machine as defcribed in plate XXII. will be found requifite; by means of the edge poft, a twig of ten or twelve inches will be in length fully fufficient for the purpofe of practice, as it is fitted into the top of the machine, which is made to fink or rife to the degree of height required. The fame range is to be allowed for this practice, as in running at the ring. The pace is to be regulated on a fimilar principle; firft, trot ten paces with the fword floped; then canter, rife in the ftirrups, and come to the *prepare.* When within twenty yards of the edge poft, bring the fword up to the *guard;* and make cut I. on the off fide as foon as within reach of it, at the fame inftant protect the

fword-

fword-arm, bring the horfe upon his haunches, and turn him to the right about.*

In like manner muft be practifed the fix cuts, and the one to the rear. The former are to be applied in the directions of the off and near fide in front.

Particular attention muft be paid to the following inftructions relative to the mode of giving edge.

Let the blade be fharpened fix inches to the point, in order that you may be able to apply it with effect, and without this precaution, it may be difficult to judge how far the edge is carried correctly.

It fhould be remembered that little force is requifite to produce effect from the application of the edge, if conducted with fkill, and that whether with a ftraight fword or fcymitar blade, no cut can be made with effect or fecurity, where the weapon does not at once free itfelf from the object to which it is applied: otherwife it muft turn in the hand, and give a contufion rather than a cut; for which reafon thofe wounds are the moft fevere, which are made neareft to the point. A fwordfman cannot therefore be too accurate in

* Until greater attention be paid in the breaking and suppling of horses than is at present shewn, caution will be required in making the sharp turns pointed out in this drill practice. It is indispensably necessary to the service of a light dragoon, that his horse should be supple and upon his haunches; the principle holds good with respect to the heavy cavalry, although the same rapidity of movement and exertion is not expected from their horses.

judging

judging the diſtance within the reach of his weapon, which can alone be done by habit and ſtrict attention.

With a scymitar not more than four or five inches of the point ſhould meet your adverſary, and ſtill leſs with a ſtraight blade, whoſe conſtruction is by no means ſo well calculated for extricating itſelf.

In coming to the poſition of the guard, direct the ſword-hand to the antagoniſt's left ear, or (in drill practice) immediately to the object at which the cut is intended to be made; keeping the hand above the level of the ſhoulder; and *as the hilt is to be a protection for the head*, at the moment the blade is in the direction of making either a *thruſt* or *cut*, it ought *never be moved from the poſition pointed out, when acting againſt cavalry ;* and as the antagoniſt changes his ground, let the ſword-hand ſhift according; but ſhould he get round to the rear, then of courſe the guard muſt give way to the modes of protecting in that direction.

Running at the ring, and giving edge, may be practiſed together with various combinations, in order to increaſe the difficulty of execution, and thereby render the ſwordſman more expert in ſkirmiſhing. This is to be done by placing edge poſts at different diſtances on each ſide of the range, to which the ſix cuts may be applied on the right and left, whilſt moving in ſpeed to give point.

Too much attention cannot be paid in attaining
perfection

perfection in the leſſons of running at the ring, and giving edge againſt infantry and cavalry; as in theſe are united horſemanſhip, and every offenſive movement which form the baſis of ſkirmiſhing.

It is not merely the ready execution of all the offenſive and defenſive movements of this ſyſtem, as practiſed under a form of exerciſe, that will render a perſon a perfect ſwordſman. Therefore in order to become a maſter of the ſword, it will be neceſſary to apply all its principles, by man oppoſing man, under certain limitations, in ſuch a way as to call forth every poſſible exertion of ſkill in individuals, both in what relates to horſemanſhip, and the uſe of the weapon; for which purpoſe the drill inſtructions will extend to the attack and defence: a mode of practice the beſt adapted to thoſe ſituations on actual ſervice in which ſoldiers are moſt likely to be engaged; as it obliges them to think for themſelves, and to act independent of each other; which on ſervice are, in a body of light troops, ineſtimable qualities. It likewiſe has the effect of training the horſes to quit the ranks readily, and the dragoons to manage them entirely with one hand; whereas at preſent, they generally employ both, unaccuſtomed as they are to manœuvre with ſwords drawn.

ATTACK

ATTACK *and* DEFENCE.

PRIOR to the attack and defence the pofitions to be oppofed to the guard (as held preparatory to an offenfive movement) fhould be perfectly underftood. This is to be acquired by the drill officer walking his horfe round his pupil in the fixt pofition termed the guard, when the recruit being ftationary, will adopt the confequent pofitions : as, for example : Suppofing the drill officer makes his approach from the rear on the near fide, the pofition to meet this would be the *bridle arm protect ;* and as the officer advances, the blade is to be brought in a progreffive degree to the *horfe near fide protect ;* and from thence carried on to the *guard*, as the officer by going round the front arrives on the off fide. At this inftant both are on the pofition termed the guard : but as the drill officer continues his round on the off fide, the dragoon will turn his body and fword hand to the right, in proportion to the movement of the officer ; and when he can no longer preferve his hand and right eye in a direct line with the left ear of his antagonift, he muft drop the point in a fmall degree to the front, in order to come to the *fword-arm protect*, without bringing the blade round the head. From the *fword-arm protect*, gradually raife the fword to the *St. George*, and continue in that pofition turning the body to the rear, obferving the movement of the officer until he arrives again on the near fide, at which time (and not before) it will be fafe to drop the blade into the pofition of *bridle arm protect*, from whence the leffon commenced.

From

From the foregoing example it muſt be obvious, that the changes of poſition in the recruit are movements adapted to meet the fixed guard of the drill officer, and that both the one and the other are only preparatory poſitions to offenſive movements, whilſt they afford protection at the moment.

It will now be proper to point out the application of thoſe movements contained in the ſix diviſions, by inſtructing the ſoldier in the principles of the attack and defence, and ſhewing him the different points of attack, and the retort to be made under the local ſituation of each movement; for which purpoſe he is to be ſeated on his horſe, and to remain ſtationary, in order to receive the attack of the drill officer, who will ride round him, making the different movements, offenſive, repeating, at the ſame time, the poſitions requiſite to be adopted for defence, which repetition may be omitted as ſoon as the eye and execution of the dragoon are ſufficiently quick to render it unneceſſary.

He is to be trained equally to attack, as to defend, and as ſoon as a ſquad is formed, they may be drawn up in two ranks, in order that the rear and front rank men may attack each other alternately, after which the practice will extend to the attack and defence in ſpeed.

At the beginning the drill officer will find it difficult to enforce a correct execution of the guards and cuts, it being frequently a fault with beginners to forget the principles of drill practice, the moment the attention becomes divided; for which reaſon more

than

than ufual care muft be taken, to fee that there is no deviation from the fyftem, which requires the arm to be kept perfectly ftraight, in order that the wrift alone may act. The edge to be correctly carried, and the protects made with the thumb fo placed as to oppofe the back of the blade to the movements of the antagonift. It fhould be an invariable rule not to fuffer an adverfary to difengage his blade immediately after a parry, unlefs it be to direct an offenfive movement, in which cafe (except he makes a feint) by parrying in the oppofite direction there is a certainty of meeting his blade.

Whenever a regiment is perfectly formed to the ufe of the fword, all practice in the modes of attack and defence may be executed with the flat and back of the blade in place of the edge. But in the firft inftance, it will be requifite for the men to be inftructed to carry the edge, for which reafon the blades of a corps may be preferved by appropriating a certain number of fwords to be made ufe of alone at the drill.

If men are taught in early practice to carry correctly the edge in performing the fix cuts, there is little danger of their being mifled by their applying the flat of the blade in the attack, particularly as the practice they muft neceffarily have in running at the edge poft, will be fufficient to confirm them in the means of carrying an edge whenever it is requifite to do fo; however fhould any perfon be found fufficiently aukward to require his being brought back to the drill practice to become correct in giving edge, it can eafily be done.

ATTACK

ATTACK *and* DEFENCE *in* LINE.

OFFENSIVE.	DEFENSIVE.
Cut I. at the horfe's head on the near fide.	The defence is, near fide proteĉt.
Cut II. at the horfe's head on the off fide.	Horfe off fide pro-teĉt.*
Cut I. at the adver-fary's face off fide. Parry cut III. by fink-ing the guard.	Left proteĉt, and re-turn cut III. at the an-tagonift's wrift.
Cut I. at the thigh or body on the off fide.	Right proteĉt, refting the hilt of the fword on the knee, when return cut VI. at the adver-fary's neck.
Parry cut VI. by the right proteĉt.	

* It may in some instances be thought expedient to carry the hanging guard round from the *near side protect* to afford a protection against cut II. at the horse on the *off side;* but it would then be found extremely difficult to come to the *left protect* in time, if after making cut II. at the horse, the antagonist should cut I. at the rider's face; and if the latter cut is parried with the point downwards, the horse-man using such guard cannot retort without his blade first taking a circular motion, during which he is exposed to cut II. In addition to the above objections, it would confine cavalry too much to a defen-sive plan, whereas their chief utility and safety consists in vigorous and systematic attack.

Make

Left Parry.

OFFENSIVE.	DEFENSIVE.
Make cut I. at the fword-arm.	Come to the fword-arm protect.
Cut II. at the bridle-arm from the rear.	Bridle-arm protect.*
Give point at the back, near fide.	Left parry.†
Cut I. at the back of the head, near fide.	Left protect.
Cut II. at the face, near fide.	Right protect.
Cut I. at the horfe's head, on the near fide.	Horfe near fide protect, and as the adverfary moves forward, return cut VI. at his fword-arm, at the fame time prefs your horfe up to his near fide and give him the point, by which the attack is changed, and he in his turn becomes on the defenfive.

* In changing from the sword-arm protect to the bridle-arm protect, press the horse with the left leg, which will throw his croup round, and by this means deprive your antagonist of that advantage of attacking you in the rear, which he would otherwise possess.

† Upon the first motion of giving point being made by the adversary, drop from the bridle-arm protect to the position requisite for parrying.

G   It

It is to be underftood that every movement, from whichfoever quarter it may proceed, is made immediately from the pofition preceding it, without firft coming to the guard between the motions.

Pursuit *on the* Near Side.

To be executed firft in a Walk, and finally in Speed.

ATTACK.	DEFENCE.
Guard.	Bridle-arm protect.
Right give point at the fmall of the back.	Left parry.
Cut I. at the back of the head.	Left protect, near fide.
Cut II. at the face.	Right protect, near fide.
Cut I. at the horfe's head on the near fide.	Horfe near fide protect.

After parrying the cut directed at the horfe's head on the near fide, return cut VI. at the antagonift's fword-arm, recovering your blade round the head in the *firft pofition* of giving point to the front, preffing your horfe at the fame inftant up to the adverfary's near fide, and give him point, which places him in his

turn

Horse near side Portrait

Plate 16   Page

No 1

No 2

No 3

No 4

EXPLANATORY PLATE

No 1

The Reg.t in line with the divisions formed in front of their respective Squadrons.

No 2

The Divisions formed upon the flanks of the Regim.t in order to perform the Exercise in Speed.

No 3

The Divisions wheel inwards forming two Lines. The dots represent the Front being extended, and ranks opened, for the attack, and defence in line.

No 4

The divisions formed for attack, & defence in Speed. The dotted line represents the filing off in the attack.

turn on the defenſive, when the ſame movements are to be repeated, as each alternately becomes the purſuer. The perſon purſued muſt be attentive in checking the pace of his horſe, in order to enable his purſuer to come eaſily up with him ; otherwiſe the object of practice would be fruſtrated, and, in place of its being a leſſon of inſtruction, it would be a trial of ſpeed between the horſes.

PART

PART III.

METHOD of INSTRUCTION

IN CLASSES.

THE whole of the *Drill Inftructions* are to be communicated to each perfon of the fquad individually; for which reafon it is neceffary to eftablifh *Claffes* and *Degrees of Progrefs in each Clafs*, into which men are to be removed according to the proficiency they make in the exercife.

There are to be three claffes, and in each clafs three degrees of progrefs.

THE FIRST *(or youngeft)* CLASS comprifes the inftructions neceffary for the foot drill, which are divided as follows :

1ft Degree. The Cuts.

2d Degree. The guards and cuts performed according to drill practice.

3d Degree.   The fword exercife performed by word
of command and fleugelmen.

THE SECOND CLASS directs the exercife on horfeback.

1ft Degree   Confifts in the opening of ranks, taking
diftances of files, and performing the
fword exercife in line.

2d Degree.   The exercife moving in circle.

3d Degree.   The exercife performed in fpeed.

THE THIRD CLASS is a general application of the
whole fyftem.

1ft Degree.   Running at the ring and giving edge.

2d Degree.   The attack and defence in line.

3d Degree.   The attack and defence in fpeed.

DIRECTIONS *to be observed with respect to the* DRILLS.

THE moft active men, and beft riders of a regiment,
are to be firft inftructed in the fword exercife, without
regard to their being non-commiffioned officers or
not.

         As

As in the 1ft and 2d degree of the firft clafs, inftruction is to be given individually to each perfon of the fquad, the fquads are never to exceed in number fix men; but in order that a regiment may be formed with the leaft delay, fquad officers muft be provided in proportion to the exertion intended, which may be readily done by means of keeping a conftant fucceffion in the *degrees of the firft clafs*, upon the principle of compound multiplication.

The following mode of employing *three men of a fquad*, the moft forward in each degree, is therefore to be followed.

The *firft man of a fquad*, who acquires a correct execution of the fix cuts, is to be immediately appointed to begin the inftruction of *three others of the regiment*.

The *fecond man* to inftruct *two*.

The *third man* to inftruct *one*.

They are to be kept thus employed until the remaining *three* men of their original fquad are completed in the 1ft *degree;* the whole fix (being the original fquad) will then be removed to the degree following, leaving fix others of their own training far advanced in their knowledge of the fix cuts, and among whom one man will always be found capable of inftructing the reft of the fquad.

Upon

Upon the fame principle are the 2d and 3d degrees of inſtruction to be conveyed, by which means the *three men moſt advanced* of each degree will be conſtantly bringing forward double their number, whilſt the aukward men of their reſpective ſquads are attaining the fame degree of knowledge with themſelves.

A regiment having the foundation of *ten formed ſwordſmen* will enter on the inſtruction of *ſixty*, which ſixty men, according to the aforeſaid ſyſtem of progreſſive drilling, will have inſtructed the like number by the time they themſelves are required to mount.

The inſtructions contained in the firſt claſs muſt be perſevered in with as little interruption as poſſible; the rudiments being eaſily forgotten, if not cloſely attended to: for which reaſon, men of the *firſt claſs* ſhould be exempted from all duties of *fatigue* and *drill*, which might otherwiſe interfere with their hours of practice.

The fame unremitting attention is not neceſſary with reſpect to the other claſſes.

Ten *days* will complete men in the *firſt claſs*—allowing them to be drilled, morning and evening, two hours each time.

The ſecond claſs will require a fortnight to perfect them for the third claſs, adhering to three hours drill per day.

The third claſs ſhould be perfectly completed in a fortnight more, by two hours drill per day only.

PART

PART IV.

———

REVIEW EXERCISE.

AT a review or infpection of a regiment of cavalry, the exercife of the fword is (after the
regiment has marched paft and formed) to precede
the evolutions, and is comprifed in the following
movements.

    I.   *The Six Divifions performed in Line.*

    II.   *The Six Divifions in Speed.*

    III.   *The Attack and Defence in Line.*

    IV.   *The Attack and Defence in Speed.*

———

THE fword exercife performed in line will be executed by the whole regiment, and the other movements by only one divifion from each fquadron.

═══════

I. *The*

I. *The* SIX DIVISIONS *performed in* LINE.

IT is not neceffary herein to fpecify the words of command, requifite to be given in order to put a regiment through the exercife; as the opening of ranks, and doubling of files, are according to the mode laid down in the drill practice, and the whole being executed by fleugelmen, the commanding officer will have only to particularize each divifion of movement, after which he will form up the doubling files, and clofe ranks.

II. *The* SIX DIVISIONS *in* SPEED.

Words of Command.

Divifions to the front form.

March.

The ranks being clofed, the divifions are to be formed by thofe men, who are previoufly appointed in each fquadron, moving forward on the *march*, forming at three horfes' lengths in front of their refpective fquadrons, and dreffing by the right.

In order to perform the exercife in fpeed, it will be requifite to form the four divifions in two lines on each flank of the regiment, with the whole fronting inwards. The two divifions of the left wing will be drawn up oppofite to the intervals of the divifions

upon

upon the right, and one fubaltern will accompany each divifion. The range between the two lines fhould not be lefs than one hundred and fifty yards, and the diftances of the divifions fufficiently great, to guard againft any poffibility of the oppofing parties riding againft each other.

Words of Command.

Ranks by threes wheel outwards.

The divifions being formed in front of the line, and told off in ranks by threes, the commanding officer will direct them to wheel outwards, and upon the word

March.

march, the two divifions of the right wing will wheel to the right, and thofe of the left in the oppo-

Halt, Drefs, March.

fite direction. As foon as they are halted, they will again get the

Trot.

words *march* and *trot*, on which they will trot off beyond the flanks of the regiment, and wheel into their new alignement.

As each divifion arrives on its ground, it is to halt, and wait for the commanding officer's order

Wheel up.

to wheel up.

Halt, Drefs.

When thus formed, the divi- fion of the third fquadron will be oppofite the interval of the two right divifions, with the fourth divifion upon its left.

On

Words of Command.	

Perform the fix divisions of movements in speed.

On receiving the caution to perform in fpeed, the right and left file of the front rank will move forwards a horfe's length in front of their refpe&ive divifions, to be in readinefs to fpring forward upon the divifion being fpecified;* at the fame time the flanks are to be kept complete, by paffaging from the center of the rank.

Firft Divifion.

The advanced files of each divifion will have their horfes well in hand, and at the word *Divifion*, move forward at an eafy gallop, increafing their fpeed gradually; each file is to dire& his horfe in a right line to the front. Thofe of the right wing, on arriving at the extremity of the range, will form to the rear of the third and fourth divifions, whilft thofe of the left wing will form in the intervals; by which means, when the exercife is completed, the four divifions will be immediately oppofite each other.†

* As the divisions are to be performed in rotation, the trumpet may be substituted for the word of command.

† The officers will accompany the last file of their divisions upon all occasions.

Attention

Words of Command.

Attention muſt be paid to regulate the time requiſite between each motion, according to the extent of ground, as every diviſion of movement ſhould begin and conclude at the oppoſite extremity of the range.

The whole are executed according to the directions given for performing the firſt diviſion.

III. *The* ATTACK *and* DEFENCE *in* LINE.

Diviſions,
Wheel inwards.

AS ſoon as the ſword exerciſe has been performed in ſpeed, the commanding officer will wheel the diviſions inwards, in order to attack and defend in line.

March.

Halt, Dreſs.

On the word *march*, the diviſions will wheel, forming two lines fronting the general; the dreſſing will finally be by the right, it will then be requiſite to extend the front of each diviſion for the purpoſe of giving the neceſſary diſtance between the files; therefore

To the center extend your front.
March.

fore on being directed to extend the front, the inner flank files will turn their horfes fronting inwards, and on the word *march*, move forward at an eafy gallop, to the center of the range, and inftantly form up, the files taking their diftance from the ftanding flank; the rear rank men will keep with their front files, and cover them exactly when formed: The divifions are to drefs by the right, forming two lines, one in the rear of the other.

Rear ranks by files to the right about turn.
March.

The rear rank will be put to the right about, in order to take the diftance of four horfes' lengths to the rear.

Forwards.
Halt, Front.

The rear files will preferve their diftances in marching to the rear fo as to cover their front rank men when fronted.

Attack and defence of the front line.

From this period the fecond line is to ftand faft till the front has gone through the whole attack and defence, and is again wheeled back to its former ground.

The

[**94**]

Words of Command.

Rear ranks,
March.

The rear rank will be in readinefs to move forward; and on the word *march* being given will advance in line at a walk, directing their horfes to the near fide of their front rank men.

Prepare to guard.

The whole of both ranks will come to the *prepare*, on receiving the word to do fo from the commanding officer, who will give it when within the diftance of fix yards from each other, and they are to be brought immediately afterwards to the *guards* applicable to their refpective fituations.

Guard.

On being ordered to guard, the rear rank will guard to the front, and the front files come to the protection of their bridle arms. The attack is to commence as in purfuit, by the rear rank giving point on the near fide, when they will execute the different offenfive and defenfive movements pointed out in drill practice for the near fide, and likewife thofe on the off fide, as far as cut I.* at the fword-arm, which being par-

* See p. 80.

ried,

| Words of Command. | ried, cut VI. is to be returned at the fword arm of the rear files, who are to retire guarding themfelves in that direction, at the diftance of a horfe's length, before they flope fwords. When the rear rank arrives on its former ground, it will halt and wait for the word to come about. |

*Files about.**   Both ranks will go to the right about, at which time the front files will face each other.

Front rank,   The front rank will move to
March.   the attack of their rear rank men directing their horfes to the off fide.

Prepare to guard.   At the diftance pointed out in
Guard.   the former attack, both ranks will be brought to the *prepare to guard,* and then the *guard.*

The attacking of the rear rank is to commence with cut II. at the horfe's head on the off fide, when all the movements in which they have already been inftructed, are to be correctly executed, con-

* By single files to the right about.

cluding

cluding with making cut I. on the near fide at the horfe, and receiving cut VI. at the fword arm. The front rank will then retire guarding the fword arm till at the diftance of a horfe's length, when they will come to the pofition of flope fwords, and halt as foon as arrived on their ground.

Rear rank take clofe order. March. The attack and defence of the firft line being ended, the rear rank will be moved up, and the files clofed.

Clofe your files. March. The divifions will clofe to their outward flanks, in order to be wheeled up to their former front.

Threes about,
Wheel outwards.
     March.
Halt, front.

The fecond line is in turn to attack and defend, which being done, the files are to be clofed, the divifions wheeled up on their own ground, and fronted, dreffing by thofe of the firft line, where they will be ready to commence their attack in fpeed.

IV. *The*

IV. *The* ATTACK *and* DEFENCE *in* SPEED.

THE attack and defence in fpeed will confift of the divifions filing fucceffively paft the general; the front and rear files attacking and defending alternately, which having done, they will return by the rear of the regiment to their places in fquadron.

────────────

Words of Command.

On receiving the order to attack and defend in fpeed, the firft divifion of the right wing will file from its left by two's, the rear file commencing the attack on the front file, according to the mode pointed out in drill practice.

Right wing, by your left, attack and defend.

March.

They are to move at a pace rather exceeding half fpeed, taking care to ride in a right line to the oppofite end of the range, where the attack will ceafe; their fwords are immediately to be floped, the files to drefs, and at a gentle trot wheel round the right flank of the regiment to their places in fquadron. The files will fucceed

H   each

Words of Command.

each other at the diftance of five horfes' lengths, till both divifions of the right wing have fucceffively rode paft the General.

Attention muft be paid, that they all move off from the fame ground which is pointed out by the leading files.

Left wing, by your right, attack and defend.

March.

The divifions of the left wing will file off from the right, and are in their turn to obferve the **rules laid down for the divifions** preceding, with this difference, that as their courfe is to be left, they will wheel round the left wing of the regiment to their places in fquadron.

J. G. L. M.

FINIS.